WE WERE HERE FIRST
THE NATIVE AMERICANS

THE
NAVAJO

Tamra Orr

PURPLE TOAD
PUBLISHING

WE WERE HERE FIRST
THE NATIVE AMERICANS

The Apache of the Southwest
The Cherokee
The Cheyenne
The Comanche
The Inuit of the Arctic
The Iroquois of the Northeast
The Lenape
The Navajo
The Nez Perce of the Pacific Northwest
The Sioux of the Great Northern Plains

Copyright © 2016 by Purple Toad Publishing, Inc.   Printing   1   2   3   4   5   6   7   8   9

Publisher's Cataloging-in-Publication Data
Orr, Tamra.
   The Navajo / written by Tamra Orr.
      p. cm.
   Includes bibliographic references and index.
   ISBN 9781624691645
1. Navajo Indians—Juvenile literature. I. Series:
We Were Here First.
   E99.N3 2016
   979.1004972
Library of Congress Control Number:
2015907815

eBook ISBN: 978-1-62469-165-2

CONTENTS

Life at Fort Sumner was brutal for many Native Americans. They were trapped and confused, and many wished for the lives they had had before.

CHAPTER 1
THE LONG WALK

It was one of the ugliest, most brutal chapters in U.S. history. Done without compassion or kindness, the event still shocks people more than 150 years later. However, once the orders had been issued, there was no turning back.

The Long Walk had begun.

In the Beginning

Brigadier General James Henry Carleton, commander of the Department of New Mexico during the Civil War, was tired of being ignored. He wanted the fame and fortune other men had earned in the war. Now he had an idea for how to get that attention. He was sure that New Mexico was brimming with gold and silver just waiting to be found, but the land was full of Native Americans. He would get rid of them—and earn the government's admiration in the process. All he had to do was make the Navajo look like the bad guys. He would blame them all for the years of murdering and robbing of settlers in New Mexico—even though these acts had been done by a few rogue Navajo, acting alone. Now, whom could he hire to hand

Carleton was eager for power and fame and was willing to do whatever he had to to accomplish it.

out the necessary punishment and make him look good?

Carleton knew just the right person—Colonel Christopher "Kit" Carson. Carson was a well-known trapper and true mountain man. He was a hero in western novels and in many newspaper headlines. If anyone could take care of the Navajo problem, it was Carson. On June 15, 1863, Carleton ordered Carson to, "with a proper military force proceed without delay to a point in the Navajoe [sic] country . . ." and

"prosecute a vigorous war upon the men of this tribe until it is considered at these Head Quarters that they have been effectually punished for their long continued atrocities."[1]

Carson was ready for the challenge of getting the Navajo off the land, but it proved harder than he had first thought. He asked the Ute, a traditional enemy of the Navajo, to help him attack the tribes. Although that helped, by August, Carson was frustrated with his lack of progress. It was time for a change.

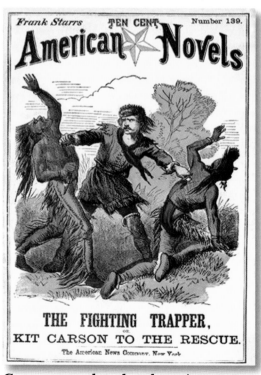

Carson was already a hero in many readers' eyes.

Carson's plan was cruel. He and his men burned every hogan, or Navajo home, they could find. They set fire to fields and orchards. They killed thousands of sheep and horses. They polluted water sources with dirt and rocks. Without food, water, homes, or livestock, thousands of Navajo had little choice but to surrender to the troops.

Carson's violent battles were often carried out in places like the Canyon de Chelly in Arizona Territory.

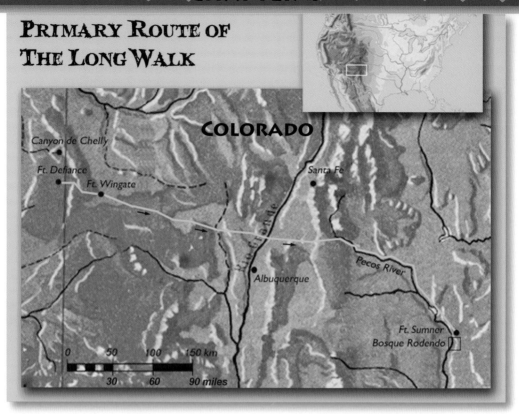

PRIMARY ROUTE OF THE LONG WALK

COLORADO

Canyon de Chelly

Ft. Defiance

Ft. Wingate

Santa Fe

Rio Grande

Albuquerque

Pecos River

Ft. Sumner
Bosque Rodendo

0   50   100   150 km

30   60   90 miles

The route the Native Americans were forced to take took them through some of the country's most beautiful—and challenging—landscape.

A Journey of Sadness

Once the Navajo surrendered, it was time to move them. In March 1864, between 8,000 and 10,000 Navajo were told they had to walk more than 400 miles to Fort Sumner in New Mexico. They were not given a choice. Carleton told Carson to say to the Native Americans:

> "Go to the Bosque Redondo [the reservation hundreds of miles away] or we will pursue and destroy you. We will not make peace with you on any other terms. . . . This war shall be pursued until you cease to exist or move. There can be no other talk on the subject."[2]

This dangerous and grueling trip became known as "The Long Walk." It was a nightmare for the Native Americans. Their moccasins, clothing, and

The Bosque Redondo Memorial at Fort Sumner celebrates the dignity, strength, and courage of the Native Americans who were forced to walk the Long Walk.

Survivors of the Long Walk at Fort Sumner. The Navajo people are the largest tribe of Native Americans in the United States. When the Navajo arrived from Canada, they came to the Four Corners: Colorado, New Mexico, Arizona, and Utah. Since then, their lives have changed dramatically. The Long Walk was a terrible moment, but their history is one of strength and survival.

blankets fell apart. They walked barefoot in snow. Many got sick from the cold weather, while others fell ill from disease or from trying to eat the unfamiliar food. Anyone who fell and did not get back up was shot or left behind. Hawks, crows, and coyotes circled the people, waiting for one to fall. Raiders attacked the long line of walkers. Many Navajo drowned while trying to cross the fast-moving Rio Grande. Hundreds died before the Navajo reached a reservation known as Bosque Redondo at Fort Sumner.

At last, the Long Walk was over for the Navajo. Those who had survived the harsh weather, starvation, and illness may have felt lucky they had reached the reservation. However, more trouble lay ahead.

Colonel Kit Carson

To countless people, Kit Carson was a national hero. He was a mountain man who seemed to do well at anything he tried. A successful hunter and trapper, he could track better than almost anyone. He was also a reliable guide. Having lived among Native Americans, he learned to speak Navajo, Apache, Cheyenne, Arapaho, Paiute, Shoshone, and Ute, in addition to Spanish and English. Even though he could not read or write, he had an incredible memory. He could especially remember geography in surprising detail.[3]

Stories about his amazing—almost superhuman—accomplishments were printed in newspapers across the country. He even starred as the hero in many Western adventure novels.[4]

Carson fought in the Mexican-American War in 1846, and then he

Carson was one of history's first celebrities, admired by many and recognized by almost all.

became a rancher. When the Civil War began, he was back on the frontier, working as an Indian agent for New Mexico. During his life, he had two Native American wives, and became a father with one.

It is hard to understand what changed Kit Carson's feelings about Native Americans. Why did this man turn into one of the leaders responsible for the death of hundreds of Navajo? Why did he force them to walk in the cold, without food, water, and clothing? Why did he not stand up for the people he once called friends? Did he ever regret his actions? No one knows, but his name will long be remembered as both hero and villain.

The Navajo were strong and lived simply, and could not understand why they had to leave the land and the life they knew best.

History talks about the Navajo tribe—but that is not really the name of this nation. The Spaniards saw the crops of corn, beans, squash, and melons the Native Americans had planted and began calling the tribe *nabaju*, or "great planted fields." The Spanish word became *Navajo*. The tribe calls itself Diné (or Dineh), meaning "The People." They came from west-central Canada to the Southwestern regions between 800 and 1,000 years ago. They traded corn and woven goods for buffalo meat and stone tools with Pueblo tribes. From other groups of people, they learned how to farm and ranch. Their lives were fairly simple and peaceful—but all of that changed when the Spanish found the tribe for the first time.

The Spaniards
In the 1600s, Spanish troops dressed in heavy metal armor moved into the area where the southwestern states of Utah, New Mexico, and Arizona are. They came in search of gold and began conquering tribes of Pueblo Indians. They forced the Native Americans into being slaves in their homes and gardens. They made them take care of their horses, sheep, and cattle.

When the Spanish arrived, they dramatically changed the lives of Native American tribes, sometimes in positive ways, but often for the worse.

Although the Pueblo fought back, they eventually lost. Many were killed or captured.

The Navajo were angry. The Pueblos were their allies. The Spaniards set their eyes to conquering the Navajo next. It was a battle that would stretch across centuries.

The arrival of the Spanish changed the lives of the Navajo in many ways. The invaders were intent on taking over, but they also brought three things with them that revolutionized the ways the Navajo lived: guns, horses, and sheep.

Three Gifts
While the Navajo did not like the Spaniards, they grew to like what the travelers brought with them. The Navajo stole many of the foreigners' guns, horses, and sheep, and quickly all three became a part of traditional life. The

guns were used to attack and defend in battle. They were also put to good use in hunting. It became possible to kill larger animals and bring back more food for the people.

The Navajo also quickly learned how to ride horses and use them as pack animals. Now the tribe could travel faster and farther. They could visit other clans and meet new traders. The horses gave them decided advantage in battles against other tribes. It also helped them escape faster when the Spaniards attacked.

Perhaps the greatest "gift" of all, however, was sheep. The Navajo became expert shepherds. They realized that these slow-moving animals were good for many things. They were a new source of meat (lamb and mutton). They provided milk. Even their wool could be used for spinning into yarn that could be woven into clothes and blankets. Sheep were sheared, or had their wool cut off, once a year. The wool was then dyed with colors made from plants, shrubs, trees, and even cacti. Sheep were used in religious ceremonies. They were given as payment. When a young man and woman were married, they were given sheep to take with them to start their homes.

Sheep provided many necessary things for the Navajo, and many tribal members become excellent shepherds.

From Spain to Mexico

In 1821, Mexico declared its independence from Spain. Suddenly, the land where the Navajo lived was not under the control of the Spaniards, but the Mexicans. It did not take long before Mexicans were leading expeditions to conquer the Native Americans. The fighting was fierce and violent. The Navajo stole livestock and took captives. By 1845, the Mexicans were losing.

In 1848, the U.S. won the war against Mexico. Mexico had to give up about half of its territory, including the area where the Navajo lived. The first thing American leaders promised the people of New Mexico was protection against the warring Navajo. Brigadier General Stephen Watts Kearny stated on August 22, "The Navajos come down from the mountains and carry off your sheep and your women whenever they please. . . . My government will correct all this."[1]

This painting of General Kearny shows him standing in the Plaza in Las Vegas. He is letting the people know that, as of August 15, 1846, New Mexico was now part of the United States.

That same year, the Navajo signed a treaty with the U.S., but it was not enough to bring peace to the two groups. The face of the Navajo's enemy simply changed once more. First, it had been the Spaniards who battled the Diné. Then it was the Mexicans. Now it was the Americans. This fight would last many years and take many lives.

A Little Lamb

Traditionally, when Navajo children were between four and six years old, they were given their own lamb to raise. The lamb's ear was carefully notched, or marked, to show to whom it belonged. Unlike the typical cat or dog, the lamb was not considered a family pet. Instead, it was property. It showed that the child was leaving youth behind and learning about adult responsibility.

Sheep were extremely important to the Navajo, and knowing how to take care of them was expected. Raising lambs took a great deal of time and dedication. The child had to be up very early in the morning to let the lamb out of the corral. Then he or she had to make sure the lamb was herded to a grassy area to graze. After hours there, the lamb had to be brought home. It was a full-time job, but it taught the children how to be part of their community.

Dorothy Begay, an adult Navajo, said during a 1981 interview, "Once we awoke in the morning, the first thing that came to our minds was herding sheep, taking out the sheep, what are the sheep going to eat. Once we had our breakfast . . . there was always someone who was going to tend the sheep. You didn't wait for someone else to do it."[2]

To the young Navajo, learning to take care of a lamb is a lesson that still continues today.

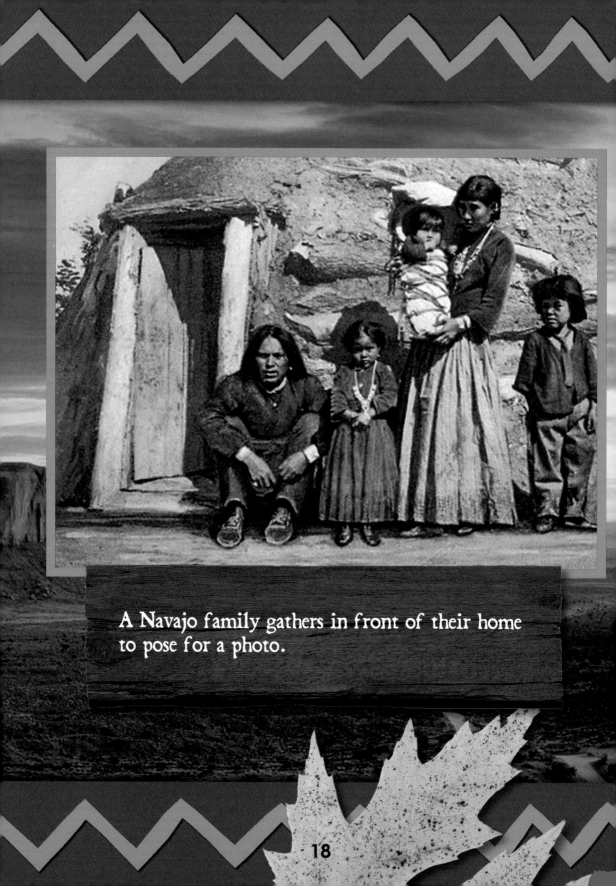

A Navajo family gathers in front of their home to pose for a photo.

CHAPTER 3
THE NAVAJO
LIFE

As the first sign of the rising sun brightens the night sky, the sun's rays hit the east-facing doorways of the Navajo hogans. Every doorway faced the same direction in order to welcome the return of the sun each morning.

Several hogans were clustered together. Each one was round and dome-shaped. The frames were made of wood, and the walls made of clay, covered in mud, weeds, and bark. A small hole in the roof let out the smoke from fires used for heating and cooking. Most doorways did not have a door, but just a woven cotton blanket to act as a barrier between inside and outside.[1]

Unlike many Native American tribes, the Navajo did not live in large villages. Instead they scattered across the territory and lived in small family groups called clans. When children married, they built a hogan close to their parents' homes so that families could stay close together.

Hogans were a single room as wide as 20 to 30 feet in diameter. They had dirt floors and no windows. The only furniture inside was bedding, typically animal skins on the floor.

While families lived in most of the hogans, other domed buildings were used for storing supplies and as sweathouses.

This re-created hogan shows how spare the interiors often were. It also shows the skill needed to fit the logs together to create the ceiling and walls.

Sweathouses were sweat baths and religious ceremonies. Although hogans were built to be temporary, they were considered more than homes. To the Navajo, they were sacred buildings. Commonly, Navajo families had two hogans—one for summer and a sturdier one for winter. They would move between them when the weather changed.

The homes and all other property, including the sheep, were owned by the women of the family. A hogan was passed down from mother to daughter. Women also did all of the farming, plus gathered nuts and fruit, while men spent their days taking care of the animals and hunting.

Before the Spaniards came to their lands, the Navajo's diet was largely corn, beans, and squash, as well as any animals they could hunt. After the foreigners came, however, the Native Americans began raising sheep. Young lambs, as well as older sheep, became main food sources. Food was prepared over a fire, either inside the hogan or out in the open air.

Navajo Boys and Girls

Long before parents had strollers or slings, Navajo women strapped their babies to long wooden cradleboards and wore them on their backs. They believed that wearing their babies introduced the children to the world around them. They also believed using cradleboards would help their babies grow straight and tall.[2] The babies were often swaddled in blankets, and a canopy was added to protect the infants from the sun and insects. A mother could slide the board off her back and lean it against a tree or wall, and her baby would still be safe.

Young boys were taught the skills of farming, taking care of animals, hunting, and tracking. Young girls were taught the skills of cooking and weaving. Boys and girls also helped by collecting firewood and working in the fields.

Coming of Age

When a Navajo girl is shifting to become an adult woman, a special ceremony called *kinaalda* is held.[3] For four days, the girl eats very little. On the first day of the ceremony, she takes a bath and then dresses in her best clothes.

The girl's best clothes and blankets are prepared for her before the ceremony starts.

The blankets are readied.

Friends and family, including the local medicine man, come to celebrate with her.

Next, the young girl lies facedown on a blanket next to her hogan. A sister or aunt then bends over her and "reshapes her." Her limbs are straightened. Her muscles are pressed down. Her hair is braided, wrapped, or knotted with *tsklólh,* or strings made of deerskin. The medicine man sings special songs.

Next, the young girl turns to the east and begins to run. She runs a quarter mile and then runs back. This short journey means that she will be strong and active for the rest of her life. She makes this run each day for four days in a row. On the last one, she is followed by any young children who are

The run begins.

After a girl officially becomes a woman, she is presented with a cake as part of the celebration.

around. This symbolizes that the girl will be a kind mother whose children will always obey her.

After the last run, a corn cake is offered to everyone at the ceremony. The young girl lets down her hair and gets to eat—now she is a woman. Soon it will be time for her to get married, a special event that is arranged by her parents.

First, the parents of the future groom propose to the parents of the future bride. If the proposal is accepted, the groom's parents put together a dowry for the bride's parents.[4] This has traditionally consisted of sheep and produce

The wedding ceremony is taken seriously in the Navajo culture. It is considered a sacred event.

grown in the fields. Weddings are performed in the couple's new hogan. A special corn mush is made by the bride's mother or grandmother and is then poured into a wedding basket and carried into the new home. The newlyweds eat the mush with their fingers. Marge Bluehorse-Anderson, who was married in a traditional Navajo ceremony in 1986, explained to *The Daily Times* why fingers are used. As her grandfather told her, "This is you and you want to go through all stages of life. You are a five-fingered being, you're an Earth surfaced person . . . and that is the make up of you."[5]

Now the new couple is ready to start their lives in their hogan. The next day, they will greet the first rays of the morning sun.

Meet the Code Talkers

Despite the U.S. government's terrible treatment of the Navajo, when Marine recruiters asked for the Navajo's help, they agreed. During World War II, secret codes were used to pass vital messages about troop movements and other top-secret details. Every time the U.S. military created a code, the Japanese found a way to break it.

Philip Johnston, a civil engineer who grew up with the Navajo, thought they could create an unbreakable code by using the Navajo language. He selected 30 young bilingual Navajo men to come with him and figure out a code. It was not easy for these Native Americans. Many had never been off the reservation. Adapting to a military lifestyle was difficult too. They had to learn to stand in line, obey barking commanders, and march endlessly.

These young men not only came up with an unbreakable code, but they learned to do so without a single error. They taught the code to others, and soon it was being used in combat. By the end of World War II, 420 Navajo men had become official code talkers.[6]

The code was updated and improved over time. It had hundreds of unique terms—but it was never written down, only spoken. Messages had to be delivered fast and be 100 percent accurate—a single error could spell disaster. The Navajo saved countless lives with their unbreakable code.

In 1971, President Richard Nixon presented the code talkers with a certificate of appreciation from the country. It thanked them for their "patriotism, resourcefulness, and courage."[7]

Navajo code talkers

The Navajo men usually let their hair grow long. Many wore it in a hair knot known as a *tsiiyeel*. Older men often added woven headbands or hats.

CHAPTER 4
THE SEARCH FOR
HOZHO

The Navajo inside the hogan were silent. All eyes were on the medicine man as he sang his sacred songs of healing. Would he be able to help the sick man lying silently on the floor?

Slowly, the medicine man gathered his supplies around him. He had a pile of crushed sandstone as well as corn pollen and charcoal from last summer's burnt trees. He made a circle of sand on the ground, almost five feet in diameter. As he chanted, the medicine man's hands kept moving. He started in the center and worked outward. A design emerged from the ground. Images of mountains appeared, along with feathers and a bright sun. Would the Yei, or Holy Ones, be pleased with the drawing? Would they reach out to the patient and bring him balance so that he could recover? The medicine man knew that if order could be restored, then all would be well, but it might take days or even weeks.

When the sand painting was done, the medicine man looked over at his patient. If the man had been well enough to move on his own, the healer would have brought him over to sit down on the circle and let the spirits from it flow into the patient. Since that was not possible, the medicine man placed his hands on the painting and then placed them on the man's

Creating intricate designs from sand and paint is still one of the Navajo's treasured art forms.

body. He continued to sing and do all he could to please the Holy Ones. Later, when the ceremony was over, the sand painting would be destroyed.

Balance and *Hozho*

In the Navajo culture, the concept of *hozho* is a guiding principle. *Hozho* is a sense of order in the world. It is the fragile combination of balance and beauty. Without *hozho,* sickness follows. Livestock may die. People may become ill. Crops could wither. Only by appealing to the gods with rituals involving special songs, stories, prayers, and paintings can balance be restored. The process sometimes takes hours to days or even weeks. Medicine men are the link between the Yei and the people. They are the ones who petition the Holy Ones to bring back order so that healing can begin.

Hozho is important in both culture and ecology. From the time the Spanish arrived, the Diné had to fight to maintain their way of life. When their homes and crops were burned and their livestock was killed, they lost all sense of balance. They either had to surrender and leave everything behind or flee into the mountains. Many of those who tried to escape were caught and added to the thousands of Navajo men, women, and children who were forced to make the Long Walk.

The Navajo who reached the reservation at Bosque Redondo in eastern New Mexico were relieved to finally stop walking—but life was not any easier. The reservation had terrible soil, so growing crops was extremely difficult. People were constantly hungry. The area was often attacked by the Comanche and other tribes. Even worse, a smallpox epidemic raced through the camp, killing thousands of people. The Navajo were miserable.

Fort Sumner was not home for the Navajo. The few who survived fought hard to hold on to their culture's ways.

The land given back to the Navajo was thick with trees and wildlife. While it was limited, it helped make it possible for the tribe to return to some of their traditions.

Heading for Home

After more than three years at the camp, the Navajo were told they could—at last—return to their homelands. A treaty between the United States and the Navajo took effect on August 12, 1868. It gave the Navajo 3.5 million acres in northeastern Arizona and northwestern New Mexico. This was only a portion of their original land, but it was better than staying at Bosque Redondo.[1]

In return for being released, the Native Americans had to agree to several new rules. They had to promise to stay within the stated boundaries of their land, to not participate in any raids, and to allow a government agent to monitor their actions. In addition, they had to allow the U.S. government to build a school and church on the grounds, and the Navajo had to attend both.

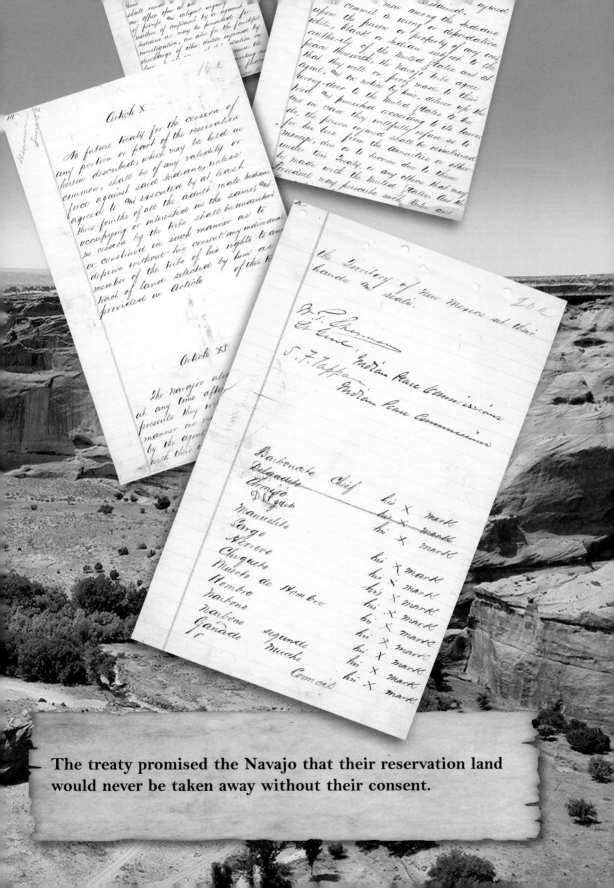

Article X

No future treaty for the cession of any portion or part of the reservation herein described, which may be held in common, shall be of any validity or force against said Indians, unless agreed to and executed by at least three-fourths of all the adult male Indians occupying or interested in the same; and no cession by the tribe shall be understood or construed in such manner as to deprive without his consent any individual member of the tribe of his rights as to any tract of land selected by him, as provided in Article ...

Article XI

The Navajo also ...
at any time after ...
presents they w... ...
manner as m... ...
by the agen... ...
with their ...

... now among the Indians ... commit a wrong or depredation upon the person or property of any one white, black or Indian subject to the authority of the United States and at peace therewith, the Navajo tribe agree that they will on proof made to their agent, and on notice by him, deliver up the wrong-doer to the United States to be tried and punished according to its laws, and in case they willfully refuse so to do, the person injured shall be reimbursed for his loss from the Annuities or other money, due or to become due to them under this Treaty, or any others that may be made with the United States. And the President may prescribe such Rules and ...

... the Territory of New Mexico set their hands and seals.

W. T. Sherman
Lt. Genl.
Indian Peace Commissioner

S. F. Tappan
Indian Peace Commissioner

Barboncito, Chief   his X mark
Delgadito   his X mark
Armijo
Delgado
Manuelito   his X mark
Largo
Herrero   his X mark
Chiqueto   his X mark
Muerto de Hombre   his X mark
Hombro   his X mark
Narbono   his X mark
Narbono segundo   his X mark
Ganado Mucho   his X mark
Cor... ...   his X mark

The treaty promised the Navajo that their reservation land would never be taken away without their consent.

On horseback, Navajo riders took time to inspect the new lands they were to call home.

The Navajo did not like these rules. They did not fit their idea of balance, but they were willing to agree if it allowed them to return to their homeland. The long walk back began, but this time it was not a brutal march at the hands of soldiers. Now, perhaps, the people would have the chance to once again find *hozho*.

Silver and Turquoise

When the Spanish came to Navajo country, the tribe's way of life changed in many ways. One skill the Native Americans learned from the Spaniards was the art of silver smithing. Silver smithing involves taking large pieces of metal and molding or hammering them into items such as dishes, candlesticks, kitchen utensils, and jewelry. The Navajo were very talented in shaping the metal. It did not take long before they began combining turquoise with silver to make rings, necklaces, and bracelets.

Turquoise is a blue-green stone made of copper and aluminum. The copper makes the stone blue. If iron is mixed in, the stone will also have touches of green. If there is also zinc in it, it will be a yellow shade. Turquoise is found in many Southwestern states, including Arizona, New Mexico, Utah, Colorado, and California.[2]

To the Navajo people, turquoise symbolizes happiness, luck, and good health. It has been used as part of religious ceremonies and traditional ceremonies. Once their jewelry became popular to trade with others, or to sell to tourists, the silversmiths began making more of it. They improved their designs as merchants and other tribes traded them better tools.

Navajo jewelry is still in high demand. It is made by hand and with quality materials. It is a reminder of years of beauty, art, and tradition.

Navajo turquoise

Navajo women often used wool blankets as
cloaks. It was common for them to decorate
their clothing with silver jewelry.

CHAPTER 5
NAVAJO
ENDURANCE

They were home at last, but life there was not as easy as the Navajo had hoped. They were under the watchful eyes of government agents. They had to send their children to school, where teachers taught students the English language and American ways, rather than the words and traditions of the Diné. The reservation was also visited by missionaries. They came to convert the Navajo to Christianity, forcing them to accept an entirely new set of beliefs.

They were not happy about any of this.

Soon, the Navajo way of life was changing in many ways. While in the past, they had largely survived by planting crops, the land they were given was not fertile. The Navajo's economy began to shift from agriculture to artwork and raising livestock. The Navajo became known not only for their jewelry, but also for their woven rugs. More and more traders traveled to the area to buy these artistic products and to set up trading posts on the reservation. The Navajo would trade their wool, rugs, baskets, sheep, and jewelry for canned goods, tobacco, coffee, flour, sugar, and tools. As important as sheep had been to the Navajo before, they were even more important now. Herds grew and grew, and slowly, so did the Navajo population.

A New Era

In 1880, the railroad came through Navajo territory. It brought a number of changes. Native American work could now be carried to distant parts of the country. In addition, the rails opened up a number of jobs for the residents of the reservation. In 1920, oil was found on the reservation. The government wanted to lease the land to get access to the oil, but the Navajo were not interested. They said no to the oil companies, so those companies sweetened the offer and said they would hire many of the Navajo to work on the project.

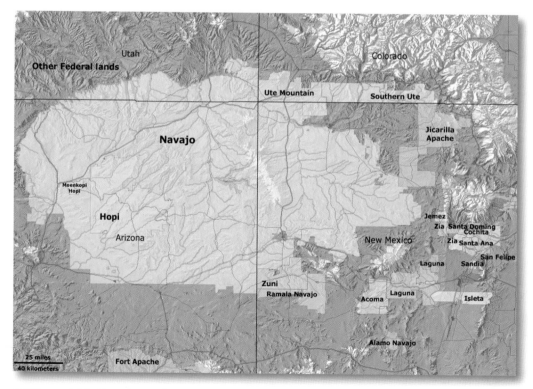

Different Native American groups scattered across the Southwest, with the Navajo taking the largest part of Utah and Colorado. This map shows the area today.

The Navajo Nation Council Chamber is located in Window Rock, Arizona. Built in 1934-1935, the building was named a National Historic Landmark in 2004.

The request to develop oil wells on the reservation did not end there, however. More and more requests came in, and the Navajo grew weary of battling each one. Finally, in 1923, a Grand Council made up of Navajo members was formed. Former Navajo chairman Peter MacDonald announced, "For the first time in the history of the Navajo Nation, the idea of a single leader was created. A twelve-member tribal council was established whose representatives were to replace the traditional extended family leaders."[1] This council would eventually be called the Navajo Nation Council. It would negotiate leases for the reservation's many natural resources, including oil, natural gas, timber, uranium, and coal.[2]

In 1934, the Navajo ran into another conflict with the government. Officials determined that the huge herds of sheep and goats were overgrazing the land and leaving behind bare ground. They told the Navajo to shrink their herds. The Navajo disagreed. They thought the answer to the problem of overgrazed land was to be given more land.[3] They wanted the boundaries of their reservation expanded. The Native Americans lost, and thousands of the animals were sold, while others were slaughtered. The Navajo were angry and frustrated.

World War II and Beyond

During World War II (1939–1945), more than 3,600 Navajo men and women enlisted. Before leaving, they took time to participate in ceremonies to safeguard them during combat. When they returned, they would hold another ceremony to help restore any balance they might have lost while in the war.

Following the war, there was more conflict. In the mid-1970s, Congress passed the Navajo-Hopi Land Settlement Act, which stuck to the rules of past treaties and divided Arizona between the Navajo and the Hopi. Once again, the Navajo lost the battle and, in 1977, nearly 3,500 Navajo were forced to relocate, while only 40 Hopi had to move.[4]

At trading posts, Navajo people enjoy chatting as they pick up things they need.

Today's Navajo

Today's Navajo live on the largest Native American reservation in the country. It covers 27,000 square miles in Arizona, Utah, and New Mexico.[5] The head of the Navajo council is in the city of Window Rock, Arizona. More than 250,000 Navajo live on this reservation. About 1,000 more live off the

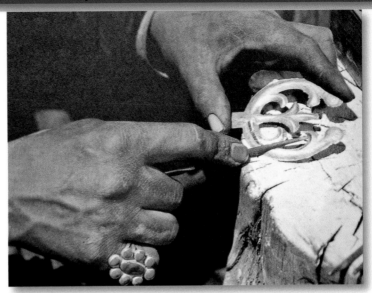

Many Navajo make a living using their hands, patience, and talent to create detailed pieces of jewelry.

reservation.[6] On the southern edge of the Mesa Verde region of the reservation is Diné College's Shiprock campus.

Decades later, the Navajo economy is still built around making jewelry, trading art, weaving rugs, and herding sheep. Many of the Navajo work in stores and other businesses throughout the reservation, and a number are also in civil service and government jobs. While some live in modern homes, there are still many hogans scattered across the reservation.

Other traditions are kept as well. About 70 percent of the Navajo speak the original tribal language at home. That is a far higher rate than in most Native American cultures. The average Native American tribe uses their tribal language only about 30 percent of the time.[7]

Preserving their language is important to many of the Navajo, although it is not always easy. In his documentary *A Seat at the Drum*, journalist Mark Anthony Rolo explains why it can be so hard to translate English into Navajo, and vice versa.

Navajo is a desert language, a language of red rock canyons, pinion pines, willows on the edges of small streams. It's a language of flash floods and scorching summer heat. It's a language of place, and the sadness of losing it is that we lose real knowledge about the desert Southwest that is thousands of years old.[8]

Monument Valley Navajo Tribal Park covers more than 91,000 acres throughout Arizona and Utah. It features sandstone towers, mesas, buttes, and trees.

The language is so important, the nation's election code requires that candidates for president and vice president be fluent in Navajo as well as in English. In 2014, Chris Deschene was disqualified from running for president because he did not pass a Navajo fluency test. Elections that year were postponed until a vote could determine how fluency would be tested.[9] On July 21, 2015, the Navajos voted to loosen the language requirements for their leaders. No longer would they have to pass a Navajo fluency test. Instead, voters would determine whether the person spoke Navajo well enough to be elected. This opened the council to having more choices in whom to elect as leaders, basing their votes on factors other than speaking the traditional language. The new rule would take effect for the 2018 Navajo Nation presidential elections.[10]

Despite the changes that come with time—and elections—the language, stories, and culture of the Navajo endure. Even as the Navajo face modern challenges, these traditions are passed to each new generation, and on into the future.

Diné College

Diné College

In 1893, one of the Navajo's greatest chiefs, Hastinn Ch'il Haajiin, told his people, "My grandchild, education is the ladder. Tell our people to take it."[11] In that spirit, the Navajo established a college in 1968 to encourage young Native American people to get an education. It was called the Navajo Community College, and it was the first college in the country established by and for Native Americans. It later changed its name to Diné College. By 2015 it had six locations in Arizona, Utah, and New Mexico. It had more than 2,000 students enrolled, and nearly 100 percent of those who apply are admitted.[12]

The philosophy of Diné College is called *"Sa'ah Naaghai Bik'eh Hozhoo."* Like the generations of Navajo from the past, this idea is that a person must live his or her life in harmony with the natural world and the universe. All courses are designed to help students learn about *nitsahakees* (thinking), *nahat'a* (planning), *lina* (living) and *sihasin* (assuring). In addition, there is a focus on learning about the Diné language, history, and culture.

Diné College has been a role model for many other tribes. Since it opened, more than 30 additional colleges have been opened by other Native American groups. Each spring, Diné College sponsors a celebration called the Pow Wow. Hundreds of dancers in full native costumes perform for visitors from many western states. Contests are held, prizes are given, and everyone has a chance to honor years of Navajo tradition.

Tribe	Navajo
Name meaning	Spanish for "great planted fields"
Cultural name	Diné, or "The People"
Culture area	American Southwest
Reservation size	27,000 square miles
Reservation population	250,000
Geography	The four corners of Utah, New Mexico, Colorado, and Arizona
Homes	Hogans
Main livestock	Sheep, goats, and horses
Main crops	Corn, squash, beans, and some fruits
Experts	Weaving rugs, clothing, and blankets; silver smithing jewelry
Primary revenue	Mining
Annual tourism	3 million people
Guiding principle	Hozho (balance)

Chapter 1

1. "The Long Walk of the Navajo," Nativeamerican.co.uk. http://www.nativeamerican.co.uk/longwalk.html

2. Raymond Friday Locke, *The Book of the Navajo* (Los Angeles: Holloway House Publishing, 2001), p. 356.

3. "December 24, 1809: Kit Carson Born in Kentucky." *This Day in History,* History.com. http://www.history.com/this-day-in-history/kit-carson-born-in-kentucky/print

4. *New Perspectives on the West*: "Kit Carson," PBS. http://www.pbs.org/weta/thewest/people/a_c/carson.htm

Chapter 2

1 "Navajo Nation: From Prehistory to the Twentieth Century," New Mexico History.org. http://newmexicohistory.org/places/navajo-nation-from-prehistory-to-the-twentieth-century

2. Teresa McCarty, *A Place to Be Navajo: Rough Rock and the Struggle for Self-Determination in Indigenous Schooling* (Mahwah NJ: Lawrence Erlbaum Associates, 2009), p. 33.

Chapter 3

1. "Navajo Homes: Hogans," NavajoPeople.org. http://navajopeople.org/navajo-hogans.htm

2. "Navajo Cradleboard Story," *Navajo Code Talkers.* http://navajocodetalkers.org/navajo-cradleboard-story/

3. "Kinaalda: Celebrating Maturity of Girls among the Navajo," *Navajo People, Culture, and History.* http://navajopeople.org/blog/kinaalda-celebrating-maturity-of-girls-among-the-navajo/

4. "Navajo Wedding Dress," *Navajo Code Talkers.* http://navajocodetalkers.org/navajo-wedding-dress/

5. Noel Lyn Smith, "Presentation Focuses on Understanding a Traditional Navajo Wedding," *The Daily Times,* April 15, 2013, http://www.daily-times.com/four_corners-news/ci_25573692/presentation-focuses-understanding-traditional-navajo-wedding

6. Jennifer Rosenberg, "Navajo Code Talkers," *About Education.* http://history1900s.about.com/od/worldwarii/a/navajacode.htm

7. "World War II: Navajo Code Talkers." HistoryNet, June 12, 2006. http://www.historynet.com/world-war-ii-navajo-code-talkers.htm

Chapter 4

1. Museum of New Mexico Office of Statewide Programs and Education, "Treaty Between the United States of America and the Navajo Tribe of Indians," History Documents. http://reta.nmsu.edu/modules/longwalk/lesson/document/treaty.htm

2. "History of Navajo Turquoise," *History of Turquoise.* http://www.historyofturquoise.com/navajo-turquoise/

Chapter 5

1. "The Navajo and Oil in the 1920s," Native American Netroots, February 14, 2012. http://nativeamericannetroots.net/diary/1257

2. "The Navajo, Sheep, and the Federal Government," Native American Netroots, November 10, 2011. http://nativeamericannetroots.net/diary/1136

3. Kathy Weiser, "Native American Legends: The Navajo Nation," *Legends of America,* January 2015. http://www.legendsofamerica.com/na-navajo.html

4. "An Historical Overview of the Navajo Relocation," *Cultural Survival.* http://www.culturalsurvival.org/publications/cultural-survival-quarterly/united-states/historical-overview-navajo-relocation

5. Wieser.

6. "Navajo: Mid 1900s to the Present." Peoples of the Mesa Verde Region. https://www.crowcanyon.org/EducationProducts/peoples_mesa_verde/today_navajo.asp

7. "Revitalizing Native Cultures." Indian Country Diaries. http://www.pbs.org/indiancountry/challenges/navajo.html

8. Ibid.

9. Alysa Landry, "Final Decision on Navajo Fluency Put to Vote July 21," *Indian Country Today*, July 6, 2015, indiancountrytodaymedianetwork.com/2015/07/06/final-decision-navajo-fluency-put-vote-july-21-160965

10. Felicia Fonseca, "Navajo Nation Loosens Language Requirements for Top Leaders," *ABC News,* July 22, 2015. http://abcnews.go.com/US/wireStory/election-focuses-navajo-language-fluency-requirement-32597567

11. "History." Diné College. http://www.dinecollege.edu/about/history.php

12. "Diné College Stats, Info and Facts." Diné College, *Cappex.* https://www.cappex.com/colleges/Diné-College

Books

Baker, Brynn. *Navajo Code Talkers*: *Secret American Indian Heroes of World War II*. Mankato, MN: Capstone Press, 2015.

Bowman, Donna Janell. *The Navajo*: *The Past and Present of the Diné*. Mankato, MN: Mankato, MN: Capstone Press, 2015.

Cunningham, Kevin, and Peter Benoit. *The Navajo*. New York: Scholastic Books, 2011.

Denetdale, Jennifer. *The Navajo*. New York:Chelsea House, 2011.

Dwyer, Helen, and D.L. Birchfield. *Navajo History and Culture*. New York: Gareth Stevens, 2012.

Iverson, Peter. *The Navajo*. New York: Chelsea House, 2006.

Santella, Andrew. *Navajo Code Talkers*. Mankato, MN: Compass Point Books. 2004.

Tieck, Sarah. *Navajo*. Mankato, MN: Big Buddy Books, 2014.

Works Consulted

"December 24, 1809: Kit Carson Born in Kentucky." *This Day in History*. History. com. http://www.history.com/this-day-in-history/kit-carson-born-in-kentucky/print

"Diné College Stats, Info and Facts." Diné College, *Cappex*. https://www.cappex.com/colleges/Diné-College

Fonseca, Felicia. "Navajo Nation Loosens Language Requirements for Top Leaders." *ABC News,* July 22, 2015. http://abcnews.go.com/US/wireStory/election-focuses-navajo-language-fluency-requirement-32597567

Fonseca, Felicia. "Navajos to Vote on Role Language Plays in Tribal Presidency." *ABC News,* July 18, 2015. http://abcnews.go.com/US/wireStory/navajos-vote-role-language-plays-tribal-presidency-32543029

"History." Diné College. http://www.dinecollege.edu/about/history.php

"History of Navajo Turquoise." *History of Turquoise*. http://www.historyofturquoise.com/navajo-turquoise/

"Kinaalda: Celebrating Maturity of Girls among the Navajo." *Navajo People, Culture and History*. http://navajopeople.org/blog/kinaalda-celebrating-maturity-of-girls-among-the-navajo/

Landry, Alysa. "Final Decision on Navajo Fluency Put to Vote July 21." *Indian Country Today,* July 6, 2015. indiancountrytodaymedianetwork.com/2015/07/06/final-decision-navajo-fluency-put-vote-july-21-160965

Locke, Raymond Friday. *The Book of the Navajo*. Los Angeles: Holloway House Publishing, 2001.

"The Long Walk of the Navajo." Nativeamerican.co.uk. http://www.nativeamerican.co.uk/longwalk.html

McCarty, Teresa. *A Place to Be Navajo: Rough Rock and the Struggle for Self-Determination in Indigenous Schooling*. Mahwah, NJ: Lawrence Erlbaum Associates, 2009.

Museum of New Mexico Office of Statewide Programs and Education. "Treaty Between the United States of America and the Navajo Tribe of Indians." History Documents. http://reta.nmsu.edu/modules/longwalk/lesson/document/treaty.htm

"The Navajo and Oil in the 1920s." *Native American Netroots*, February 14 ,2012. http://nativeamericannetroots.net/diary/1257

"Navajo Cradleboard Story." *Navajo Code Talkers.* http://navajocodetalkers.org/navajo-cradleboard-story/

"Navajo Homes: Hogans." NavajoPeople.org. http://navajopeople.org/navajo-hogans.htm

"Navajo: Mid 1900s to the Present." *Peoples of the Mesa Verde* Region. https://www.crowcanyon.org/EducationProducts/peoples_mesa_verde/today_navajo.asp

"Navajo Nation: From Prehistory to the Twentieth Century." New Mexico History.org. http://newmexicohistory.org/places/navajo-nation-from-prehistory-to-the-twentieth-century

"The Navajo, Sheep, and the Federal Government." *Native American Netroots,* November 10, 2011. http://nativeamericannetroots.net/diary/1136

"Navajo Wedding Dress." *Navajo Code Talkers.* http://navajocodetalkers.org/navajo-wedding-dress/

"Revitalizing Native Cultures." Indian Country Diaries. http://www.pbs.org/indiancountry/challenges/navajo.html

Rosenberg, Jennifer. "Navajo Code Talkers." *About Education.* http://history1900s.about.com/od/worldwarii/a/navajacode.htm

Smith, Noel Lyn. "Presentation Focuses on Understanding a Traditional Navajo Wedding." *The Daily Times,* April 15, 2013. http://www.daily-times.com/four_corners-news/ci_25573692/presentation-focuses-understanding-traditional-navajo-wedding

Weiser, Kathy. "Native American Legends: The Navajo Nation." *Legends of America,* January 2015. http://www.legendsofamerica.com/na-navajo.html

"World War II: Navajo Code Talkers." HistoryNet, June 12, 2006. http://www.historynet.com/world-war-ii-navajo-code-talkers.htm

On the Internet

Native Americans: Navajo Tribe from Ducksters
    http://www.ducksters.com/history/native_american_navajo.php

Native American Facts for Kids: Navajo Indian Fact Sheet
    http://www.bigorrin.org/navajo_kids.htm

Navajo Nation for Kids from Mr. Nussbaum
    http://mrnussbaum.com/navajo/

Navajo Tribe from Kidport Reference Library
    http://www.kidport.com/reflib/usahistory/NativeAmericans/Navajo.htm

ally (AL-ly)—A friend or partner.

atrocity (uh-TRAH-sih-tee)—A cruel or violent act; a horrifying event.

bilingual (by-LING-wul)—Able to speak two languages fluently.

convert (kun-VERT)—To change from one belief to another.

epidemic (eh-pih-DEH-mik)—Describing a disease that spreads quickly and infects a lot of people at the same time.

expedition (ek-speh-DIH-shun)—A great journey, usually taken in order to explore.

fertile (FER-tul)—Able to support crops.

hogan (HOH-gun)—A dome-shaped Navajo home.

missionary (MIH-shuh-nayr-ee)—A person sent by a church to spread religion.

mutton (MUH-tun)—Meat from adult sheep.

negotiate (neh-GOH-shee-ayt)—To reach an agreement through formal talks.

overgraze (OH-ver-grayz)—To allow animals to crop too much of a land's grasses or grains.

petition (peh-TIH-shun)—A formal request made to a god or a king.

relocate (ree-LOH-kayt)—To move to a different home.

reservation (reh-zer-VAY-shun)—A piece of public land set aside for a specific group of people.

revolutionize (reh-vuh-loo-shuh-nyz)—To bring about a positive change.

sweathouse (SWET-hows)—A spiritual building for sweating in order to cleanse the body and spirit.

trapper (TRAP-er)—A person who hunts using traps.

treaty (TREE-tee)—An official agreement.

MEET THE
AUTHOR

Tamra Orr is the author of more than 400 nonfiction books for readers of all ages. She lives in the Pacific Northwest with her husband and children. She graduated from Ball State University and has been writing ever since. When Orr is not researching and writing a book, she is writing letters, reading books, and camping in the incredibly beautiful state of Oregon.